Searchlight
BOOKS™

What Can
We Do about
Pollution?

How Can We Reduce

Manufacturing
Pollution?

Douglas Hustad

Lerner Publications ◆ Minneapolis

Copyright © 2016 by Lerner Publishing Group, Inc.

Content Consultant: Roopali Phadke, Associate Professor of Environmental Studies, Macalester College

Lerner Publications Company
A division of Lerner Publishing Group, Inc.
241 First Avenue North
Minneapolis, MN 55401 USA

For reading levels and more information, look up this title at www.lernerbooks.com.

Library of Congress Cataloging-in-Publication Data

Hustad, Douglas.
  How can we reduce manufacturing pollution? / by Douglas Hustad.
     pages cm. — (Searchlight books. What can we do about pollution?)
  Audience: Age 8-10.
  Audience: Grade 4 to 6.
  Includes bibliographical references and index.
  ISBN 978-1-4677-9518-0 (lb : alk. paper) — ISBN 978-1-4677-9703-0 (pb : alk. paper) — ISBN 978-1-4677-9704-7 (eb pdf)
1. Manufacturing processes—Waste minimization—Juvenile literature. 2. Lean manufacturing—Juvenile literature. 3. Waste minimization—Juvenile literature. 4. Air—Pollution—Prevention—Juvenile literature. 5. Water—Pollution—Prevention—Juvenile literature. 6. Soil pollution—Prevention—Juvenile literature. I. Title.
  TS169.H87 2016
  628.1'6837—dc23
                        2015027076

Manufactured in the United States of America
1 – VP – 12/31/15

Contents

Chapter 1

MANUFACTURING POLLUTION

Factories manufacture, or make, many of the important products we use every day. But these products come with side effects. Manufacturing pollution is all the harmful waste that factories produce while making things.

Some factories manufacture clothing. What is manufacturing pollution?

Chapter 2

AIR POLLUTION

A normal adult breathes more than 3,000 gallons (11,000 liters) of air every day. That's about 2 gallons (8 liters) of air every minute! Unfortunately, manufacturing can affect how clean the air is.

In some places, people wear masks because the air pollution is so bad. How much air does an adult breathe every day?

When factories heat up certain materials, they produce gases. These gases then get into the air. For example, oil refineries are places that make products out of oil. This process creates a gas called sulfur dioxide.

Factories also need electricity to manufacture things. To generate this electricity, many factories burn coal or diesel fuel. This produces a gas called carbon dioxide.

OIL REFINERIES MAKE PRODUCTS
SUCH AS GASOLINE AND DIESEL FUEL.

After goods are manufactured, they must be transported to stores. This is usually done by train, truck, ship, or airplane. Like the factories, these vehicles burn fuel. This produces even more carbon dioxide.

Semi trucks deliver many of the products we use. But they also put pollution into the atmosphere.

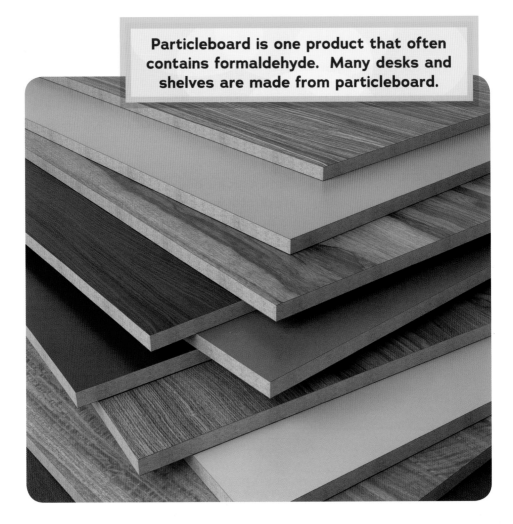

Particleboard is one product that often contains formaldehyde. Many desks and shelves are made from particleboard.

Pollution does not always stop when the manufacturing is done. Completed products can still pollute. One example is formaldehyde. This chemical is used in flooring and other wood products. At room temperature, these products can release a toxic gas into the air. This process is called off-gassing.

Effects of Air Pollution

Polluted air can cause breathing problems for people and animals. It can also irritate their skin and eyes. People with asthma, a lung disorder that makes it hard to breathe, are the most at risk. If someone is exposed to air pollution for a long time, the effects can be more serious. For example, formaldehyde can cause throat cancer and lung cancer. Sulfur dioxide can cause lung disease and heart disease.

People with asthma sometimes have to use inhalers to help them breathe.

Sulfur dioxide also causes acid rain. This toxic rain is harmful to plants and animals. It can damage buildings too.

Carbon dioxide traps heat inside Earth's atmosphere. Too much of this gas causes our planet to get warmer. And these warmer temperatures lead to climate change.

Climate change can lead to melting ice in the polar regions. This causes sea levels to rise. People who live near coasts may have to move.

President George H. W. Bush signed the Clean Air Act of 1990 to limit air pollution from factories.

Solutions to Air Pollution

Once harmful materials get into the air, they are nearly impossible to clean up. So the Environmental Protection Agency (EPA) works to prevent pollution. In 1970, the US Congress passed the Clean Air Act. This law sets limits on the amounts of toxic chemicals that can be released. The law was expanded in 1990 and now does even more. The Clean Air Act and others like it have helped reduce the damage caused by manufacturing pollution.

A worker directs the installation of a scrubber at an oil refinery.

New technology has also helped. Air cleaners called scrubbers can be added to smokestacks. They remove many harmful toxins from the smoke.

Anything a manufacturer puts into the air, harmful or not, is called an emission. Since 1970, emissions of the six most common pollutants have gone down 68 percent. Between 1980 and 2010, emissions of sulfur dioxide fell by 76 percent.

Chapter 3

WATER POLLUTION

Like the air we breathe, water is essential for life. Some manufacturing processes use water too. Fabric and paper manufacturing are two examples.

This machine uses water to make paper out of wood pulp. What other manufacturing processes use water?

FACTORIES SOMETIMES SEND POLLUTED
WATER INTO LAKES AND RIVERS.

But these processes use more than water. They also use chemicals, including benzene and chlorine. Some of these harmful materials get into the water during manufacturing. Afterward, the leftover water has to be disposed of. Some of it is poured into rivers or kept in storage ponds.

Polluted water may also drain into sewers. Older cities often have combined sewer systems. That means a factory's wastewater will mix with rain runoff from the city's gutters in a single sewer pipe. In heavy rains, these sewers can overflow. The polluted water then flows into nearby rivers, lakes, or oceans.

A sewer overflows after a large storm.

Firefighters try to put out a fire on the Cuyahoga River in 1952.

What Effects Does Water Pollution Have?

Chlorine and benzene can poison drinking water. These chemicals are also harmful to fish and other wildlife. For example, the Cuyahoga River in Cleveland, Ohio, became very polluted in the mid-1900s. Chemicals had been dumped into the river for decades. No fish could survive. The pollution got so bad that the river caught fire!

Chemicals can also make rivers and lakes unsafe for swimming or fishing. Polluted water is hard to clean. And the cleaning process can be very expensive.

A SIGN WARNS PEOPLE THAT THE WATER IS TOO POLLUTED FOR SWIMMING.

What Are the Solutions to Water Pollution?

Cities are replacing combined sewer systems with separate sewer systems. That means factories have sewers that take wastewater to a plant to be cleaned first. Runoff has its own separate sewer.

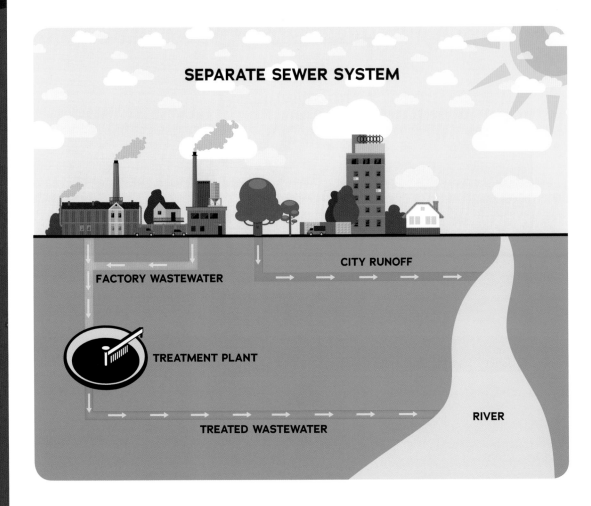

SEPARATE SEWER SYSTEM

FACTORY WASTEWATER

CITY RUNOFF

TREATMENT PLANT

TREATED WASTEWATER

RIVER

At a wastewater treatment plant, water goes into settling tanks where pollutants are removed.

The Clean Water Act of 1972 sets limits on what factories can release. It also requires that factories have a permit before releasing anything into a body of water. Companies face penalties for not having a permit.

The EPA decides how much treatment of the water is necessary. Wastewater gets cleaned at a treatment plant until it is safe enough to be released. The plant removes pollutants and disinfects the water.

The Cuyahoga River has not had a fire since 1969.

Water pollution remains a problem. But people are making progress. Rivers such as the Cuyahoga are much cleaner than they were fifty years ago. Today, bald eagles nest on the Cuyahoga's shores. Other fish and wildlife are starting to come back as well.

Chapter 4

SOIL POLLUTION

Soil pollution can happen all at once or slowly over time. The cause could be a large, accidental spill of chemicals. Or it could be a slow chemical leak from a storage tank.

A train crash could cause chemicals to spill onto the soil. What is another way that soil can become polluted?

Many factories bury their waste. But sometimes this waste is not properly contained. When this happens, hazardous materials can leak into the soil.

Soil pollution is also connected to air and water pollution. For example, pollution from the air can settle on land, harming the soil. Contaminated, or polluted, soil can also leak chemicals into underground water supplies.

A factory illegally dumped these barrels full of toxic waste.

Farmers' crops may become contaminated by toxic chemicals in the soil.

Soil Pollution Effects

Polluted soil can cause a chain reaction. Toxic chemicals may prevent plants from growing in the soil. The plants that do grow are contaminated. Then humans or animals eat the contaminated plants. Also, kids could play in the dirt. When that happens, they may breathe it in or accidentally eat it. So, people and animals can consume toxins without even knowing it.

If soil has contaminated the groundwater, that water is no longer safe to drink. Soil or water that has been polluted can cause health problems. Consuming water or food from contaminated soil can cause food poisoning in the short term. In the long term, it can cause cancer and birth defects.

A scientist takes a soil sample to test for pollution.

Soil Pollution Solutions

Like air pollution and water pollution, soil pollution is hard to clean up. But there are a few ways it can be done. After the soil is dug up, it can be treated with chemicals and replaced. It can also be disposed of. Usually this means burning the soil or safely burying it. But this solution is not perfect. Burning the soil can put the pollution into the air instead.

Contaminated soil is put into bags. It will be carried away and burned.

Pumpkin plants can suck toxins out of the dirt. They were used to clean up polluted soil near a factory that made markers.

Sometimes soil can be cleaned in place. Scientists have ways of breaking down harmful substances to safe levels. This process uses natural organisms that attack the pollutants. Scientists are also doing experiments with certain plants that absorb chemicals.

The pollution can also be contained so it will not hurt anything. But this does not clean the soil at all. If the containers break, pollution happens all over again.

All these methods have problems. It is difficult to clean up the soil without creating other pollution. And cleanup is expensive. Companies face fines for accidental spills. The best way to deal with soil pollution is to prevent it from happening in the first place. Manufacturers are now working harder to control waste and prevent accidents.

Many car factories are now recycling their waste.

Chapter 5

WHAT CAN YOU DO?

Factories make lots of great products that people love. But it is important to know how manufacturing affects our environment. One person alone cannot control how companies do their manufacturing. But together, people can have a big impact on what companies make and how they make it.

Workers assemble electronics in a factory. How can people reduce the amount of pollution factories create?

Start by trying to reduce the amount of stuff you buy. If people buy less stuff, companies will make less stuff. That means factories will use less energy and create less pollution.

One way to buy less stuff is to reuse products. Rather than buying new items, try to reuse things until they wear out. You can also borrow things from friends instead of buying new items.

Consider using secondhand sports equipment instead of buying new items.

Many things can be recycled, including plastic, glass, metal, and paper.

Recycling is another way to reduce manufacturing pollution. For example, it takes less energy to make cans and bottles from recycled materials than to make new ones. So, it's a good idea to recycle whatever you can.

You might be surprised how many products can be made from recyclable materials. Fleece jackets and carpet can be made from plastic bottles. Soup cans may be turned into parts for bikes or cars.

Of course, sometimes you have to buy new things. When you do, choose products made from recycled materials if possible. You can also look for products with less packaging. More packaging means more energy was used to produce it.

Instead of buying foods packaged in plastic and Styrofoam, look for foods that are sold without packaging.

It also helps to stay informed. Be sure to buy products from companies that manufacture responsibly. One thing to look for is the Forest Stewardship Council (FSC) logo. It means the product was made responsibly. One product you can find it on is paper. Paper factories use a lot of water and chemicals. The FSC logo means the manufacturer protected the environment while making that paper.

A worker puts the FSC logo on a tree trunk.

You can also ask an adult for help. Stay involved with environmental events around you. Help clean up a polluted site. And tell others about what they can do. The more we reduce manufacturing pollution, the brighter the future will be!

Glossary

atmosphere: all of the air that surrounds Earth

by-product: a material left over by the manufacturing process

contaminated: polluted

disinfect: to clean something by destroying harmful substances in it

emission: air toxins generated by manufacturing

factory: a place where things are made

manufacture: to make something, often with machines

off-gassing: a process in which products release toxic gas after they are manufactured

pollutant: any substance that contributes to pollution

raw materials: basic substances that have not yet been made into goods. Raw materials include coal, logs, crude oil, and iron ore.

runoff: water that flows over the surface rather than soaking into the ground

sewer: a channel that carries away wastewater, usually underground

toxic: harmful or poisonous

Learn More about Manufacturing Pollution

Books

Flounders, Anne. *Reducing Waste*. South Egremont, MA: Red Chair Press, 2014. Colorful photos and interesting facts make this book a must-read.

Ostopowich, Melanie. *Water Pollution*. New York: AV2 by Weigl, 2010. This book helps readers understand the effects of water pollution.

Rapp, Valerie. *Protecting Earth's Land*. Minneapolis: Lerner, 2009. This fascinating book explores the harm being done to Earth's land and what readers can do to help.

Websites

EPA: Acid Rain
http://www.epa.gov/acidrain/education/site_students/
The games and activities on this website provide lots of important information about acid rain.

NIEHS Kids' Pages: Pollution
http://kids.niehs.nih.gov/explore/pollute/index.htm
This website offers lots of facts about pollution, including ideas for prevention.

PBS Kids: The Greens
http://meetthegreens.pbskids.org/
This site features games and videos that help students learn about reducing the amount of stuff they buy.

Index

Photo Acknowledgments

The images in this book are used with the permission of: © kzenon/iStockphoto, p. 4; © Darinburt/ iStockphoto, p. 5; © tellmemore000/iStockphoto, p. 6; © Ilona Koeleman/Shutterstock Images, p. 7; © Askold Romanov/iStockphoto, p. 8 (right); © mir vam/Shutterstock Images, p. 8 (left); © Hung Chung Chih/Shutterstock Images, p. 9; © EasyBuy4u/iStockphoto, p. 10; © DarthArt/iStockphoto, p. 11; © Axe Olga/iStockphoto, p. 12; © moodboard/Thinkstock, p. 13; © Dhoxax/iStockphoto, p. 14; © Charles Tasnadi/AP Images, p. 15; © Mead Gruver/AP Images, p. 16; © Li Chaoshu/Shutterstock Images, p. 17; © Tim-e/iStockphoto, p. 18; © Dizzy/iStockphoto, p. 19; © Bettmann/Corbis, p. 20; © Joseph Sohm/Shutterstock Images, p. 21; © Bukhavets Mikhail/Shutterstock Images, p. 22 (top); © angelh/Shutterstock Images, p. 22 (bottom); © Mihail Dechev/iStockphoto, p. 23; © Patricia Elaine Thomas/Shutterstock Images, p. 24; © Jerry Sharp/Shutterstock Images, p. 25; © Karnt Thassanaphak/Shutterstock Images, p. 26; © Gomez David/iStockphoto, p. 27; © AlexKZ/ Shutterstock Images, p. 28; © Keith Dannemiller/Corbis, p. 29; © nano/iStockphoto, p. 30; © Rainer Plendl/iStockphoto, p. 31; © Ed Stock/iStockphoto, p. 32; © Cindy Singleton/iStockphoto, p. 33; © Hurst Photo/Shutterstock Images, p. 34; © promicrostockraw/iStockphoto, p. 35 (right); © Kivilcim Pinar/iStockphoto, p. 35 (left); © Oliver Berg/Picture-Alliance/DPA/AP Images, p. 36; © Mark Bowden/iStockphoto, p. 37.

Front Cover: © M. Shcherbyna/Shutterstock.com

Main body text set in Adrianna Regular 14/20.
Typeface provided by Chank.